SWU-600-002

DUTCH & IMPERIAL SOLDIERS

✧

BY ADAM VAN BREEN & HENDRICK GOLTZIUS

Series curated by
Luca Stefano Cristini

SOLDIERSHOP PUBLISHING

AUTHOR

Adam Van Breen (1585-1642) Dutch renommated artist and engraver was born in Amsterdam and specialized in winter landscapes. He became a member of the Hague Guild of Saint Luke in 1612 and besides the Hague is known to have worked in Amsterdam and Oslo.He died in Norway. His series of military Dutch Nassau soldiers, subjets of our book is widely known.

Hendrick Goltzius (1558 – 1617), was a German-born Dutch printmaker, draftsman, and painter. He was the leading Dutch engraver of the early Baroque period, or Northern Mannerism, noted for his sophisticated technique and the "exuberance" of his compositions. According to A. Hyatt Mayor, Goltzius "was the last professional engraver who drew with the authority of a good painter and the last who invented many pictures for others to copy". In middle age he also began to produce paintings.

To my father Amilcare

Title: **DUTCH & IMPERIAL SOLDIERS - by Adam Van Breen & Hendrick Goltzius**
Series edit & curated by Luca S. Cristini. First edition by Soldiershop. November 2016
Cover & Art Design: Luca S. Cristini. Plates re-colorations by Anna Cristini.
ISBN code: 978-88-93271547 Code SWU-600-002
Published by Soldiershop publishing, via Padre Davide, 7 - 24050 Zanica (BG) ITALY. www.soldiershop.com
On cover two pikemen from the Van Breen series.

DUTCH &

IMPERIAL SOLDIERS

BY ADAM VAN BREEN &
HENDRICK GOLTZIUS

THE MILITARY EVOLUTIONS OF THE PRINCE OF NASSAU
IN THE ART OF ADAM VAN BREEN AND HENDRICK GOLTZIUS

The famous German-Dutch artists Adam Van Breen and Hendrick Goltzius also put their considerable talents to use in creating several works based on military subjects. All the colour plates from Adam van Breen's illustrated work, *"The military evolutions of the Prince of Nassau"*, 1617, are presented for the first time in this book.

About 50 handsome copper engravings magnificently portray the step-by-step sequence for training foot soldiers in handling the standard weaponry of 17th century warfare: exercises with sword, pike and shield.

The second part focuses on Hendrick Goltzius' work, based on 26 men at arms, also know as Rudolph's army soldiers. These illustrations are all presented for the first time in full colour!

This book complements the first volume already published on Jacob de Gheyn, *"The Exercise of Armes"*.

A third is in production, dealing with cavalry and knights from the same period, as depicted by great Dutch artists.

The three volumes will present a meticulously accurate depiction of period uniforms and weapons from the Netherlands and Europe, with the additional aesthetic appeal of remarkable engravings by these great artists !

◀ *Portrait of Willem Jansz. Cock, standard-bearer of the Orange Vendel militia of the Hague (1617) by Everard Quirijnsz. Van der Maes.*

CONTENTS

VAN BREEN "DE EXERCITIE MET DE TARGE EN RAPIER"
(THE EXERCISE WITH SWORD AND SHIELD)

The end of the sixteenth century saw a revival of interest in the military writings of the Romans. Translations of these works and studies of them, made their way to the commanders of the armies of the Northern Netherlands, causing the Frisian stadholder William Louis of Nassau, his brother John, and their cousin Prince Maurice to reorganise the armies under their command according to the Roman model. By thus standardising commands and instructions they managed to transform the motley mercenary troops with whom they had to fight the unequal battle against Spanish-Parma's regiments, into a well-disciplined army, ready for battle.

From preserved lists of standard commands in various languages we can see clearly the thorough approach of it all. Instructions on the use of weapons were, moreover, accompanied by explanatory illustrations. The best known example, also internationally, is the *"Wapenhandelinghe van roers, musquetten ende spiesen"*, well know as: *"The Exercises of armes"* depicted by Jacob de Gheijn.

Less well-known, but by no means less beautiful is the book from which all the colour plates is reproduced here: Adam van Breen's *"Nassausche wapen-handelinge, van schilt, spies, rappier, ende targe"*. The written instruction accompanying the illustrationes gives as the starting position: for example: *"He shall carry his shield on his back and nowhere else, and put the lance beside his right foot, his arm not outstretched but bent, so as to facilitate holding the lance to his side when the ranks are closed"*.

All the illustrations was designed by the painter Adam van Breen, who was working in The Hague from 1611 to c. 1618, and had his drawings engraved by various artists. On 8 December 1617 he sold the copperplates to the Hague printer and bookseller Aert Meuris, who wanted to publish them in book form. When it was published it only bore the name of Van Breen, without the imprint of Aert Meuris.

There is a painting by Van Breen (now at the Rijksmuseum in Amsterdam) portraying Prince Maurice and Prince Frederick Henry walking along Korte Vijverberg in The Hague. Van Breen must therefore have been in contact with the Oranges, and he has presented his *Wapenhandelinge* to Prince Maurice himself. The copy that we have use in our book is now part of the collection of Rijksmuseum Library of Amsterdam.

ADAM VAN BREEN

He was born probably around 1585 in Amsterdam and specialized in winter landscapes. He became a member of the Hague Guild of St. Luke (*Lukasgilde)* in 1612, until 1621 and besides the Hague is known to have worked in Amsterdam and Oslo.

He died in Norway after 1642.

He is a renomated Dutch painter and engraver active in Holland from 1611 to 1640. Belonging to the same generation of Hendrick Avercamp (the pioneer of this type of painting), Adriaen van de Venne, Arentsz and Arent, Adam van Breen contributed to the success of winter scenes (*Wintertje*) of Flemish origin, suggestive of skaters on frozen canals and rivers in a setting of trees and houses.

Adam van Breen is now considered as one of the finest specialists of these seasonal landscapes, depicting the pleasures of games played on ice by elegant characters from high society.

In 1611, in The Hague, Adam van Breen married Maria Gelle.

In 1624 he was in Christiana (Denmark), then in 1628 again in Amsterdam.

In 1636, he returned to Norway, where he participates in decorations of Akershus Castle. Adam van Breen in 1617 illustrated *"The military evolutions of the Prince of Nassau"* that we present complete color plates in this book.

▲ *Stadtholder Maurice of Nassau with his Bodyguard and Entourage at the Frozen Hofvijver in The Hague, 1618. Paint by Adam van Breen*

HENDRICK GOLTZIUS

Hendrick Goltzius (1558 –1617), was a German-born Dutch printmaker, draftsman, and painter. He was the leading Dutch engraver of the early Baroque period, or Northern Mannerism, noted for his sophisticated technique and the "exuberance" of his compositions. According to A. Hyatt Mayor, Goltzius *"was the last professional engraver who drew with the authority of a good painter and the last who invented many pictures for others to copy"*.

In middle age he also began to produce paintings. Most famous Dutch artist as De Gheyn, Van Breen and others were pupils of Goltzius.

Biography

Goltzius was born near Venlo in Bracht or Millebrecht, a village then in the Duchy of Julich, now in the municipality

▲ *Hendrick Goltzius Self-Portrait 1593 about*

Brüggen in North Rhine-Westphalia. His family moved to Duisburg when he was 3 years old. After studying painting on glass for some years under his father, he learned engraving from the Dutch polymath Dirck Volckertszoon Coornhert, who then lived in Cleves. In 1577 he moved with Coornhert to Haarlem in the Dutch Republic, where he remained based for the rest of his life. In the same town, he was also employed by Philip Galle to engrave a set of prints of the history of Lucretia.

Goltzius had a malformed right hand from a fire when he was a children, which turned out to be especially well-suited to holding the burin; *"by being forced to draw with the large muscles of his arm and shoulder, he mastered a commanding swing of line"*.

In the 1580s, Goltzius with his friends van Mander and the painter Cornelis van Haarlem, founded an art academy in Haarlem in emulation of those in France and Bologna, where the human figure could be studied from life and to provide a meeting-place for artists to discuss both practice and aesthetics.

At the age of 21 he married a widow somewhat advanced in years, whose money enabled him to establish an independent business at Haarlem; but his unpleasant relations with her so affected his health that he found it advisable in 1590 to make a tour through Germany to Italy, where he acquired an intense admiration for the works of Michelangelo. He returned to Haarlem in August 1591, considerably improved in health, and worked there until his death.

Jamais Faille

10

His portraits, though mostly miniatures, are masterpieces of their kind, both on account of their exquisite finish, and as fine studies of individual character. Of his larger heads, his life-size self-portrait is probably the most striking example.

Goltzius brought to an unprecedented level the use of the *"swelling line"*, where the burin is manipulated to make lines thicker or thinner to create a tonal effect from a distance. He also was a pioneer of *"dot and lozenge"* technique, where dots are placed in the middle of lozenge shaped spaces created by cross-hatching to further refine tonal shading.

▲ *Hendrick Goltzius Self-Portrait 1593 about*

Hollstein credits 388 prints to him, with a further 574 by other printmakers after his designs. In his command of the burin, Goltzius is said to rival Dürer. He made engravings of Bartholomeus Spranger's paintings, thus increasing the fame of the latter – and his own. Goltzius began painting at the age of forty-two; some of his paintings can be found in Vienna. He also executed a few chiaroscuro woodcuts. He was the stepfather of engraver Jacob Matham. He died, aged 58, in Haarlem.

Van Mander and Goltiuz

The painter, poet and writer of the famous Schilder-boeck, Karel van Mander (Meulebeke 1548 - 1606 Haarlem) was one of the major designers of prints in Holland between 1587 and 1606. He produced several important designs. The range of subjects, however is more varied than that found in Goltzius's oeuvre. It contains mainly biblical subjects, mythological themes and allegories and secular subjects such as proverbs and peasant scenes, blazons and book-titles. In addition there is one portrait which falls into a subject category denigrated by Van Mander as a 'sideline' of the art. The engravers of Karel van Mander's designs all came from or were in some way connected to the Goltzius workshop of the late 1580s. Goltzius's stepson Jacob Matham, Jacques de Gheyn, and Jan Saenredam were his pupils. Jan Muller frequented the workshop during that period. Goltzius also apprenticed the more obscure engravers Nicolaes Clock, Gillis van Breen, Nicolaes Braeu and Cornelis Drebbel. Although most of them continued to work for Goltzius during the 1590s, their engravings after Karel van Mander seem to have been produced independently.

◄ *Portrait of Jacques de la Faille (1548-1615), Colonel Antwerp vigilante after 1584 merchant in Haarlem. Standing, turned to the left, right hand leaning on helmet, left hand on sword. Name dressed. In oval without edge lettering. Counterpart portrait of wife Josina Hamels. Paint by Hendrick Goltzius*

GOLTIUZ MEN AT ARMS (notes to color plates)

1) P.68 -1582 Infantry capitain : Portrait of a man (probably) a partisan (pole weapon) in his right hand. Previously also identified as Jan Dircksz. Estimator, captain Haarlem. Right to a tree stump a shield with a flower on it and the slogan 'Hodie: Cras nil' underneath. In the background a battle. Among the show a four-line Latin poem

2) P.69- From beginning of the 16th century, good posture dictated That the shoulders shouldering be thrown back and the breast thrust out. This contemporary ideal of beauty was Emphasized by padding the front of the doublet, creating a Peascod belly. Goltzius and the Gheyn exploited this fashion to make Their officers appearacne more courageous and combative. In the foreground to see the standard-bearer in the background is the city of Haarlem. Counterpart to the post of captain of the infantry from 1587.

3) P.70- A man with a pointed weapon (partisan) in the right hand, in a nutshell. In the background infantry troops. Among the show two lines of text in Latin. This print is part of a series of three military officers.

4) P.71- In the foreground the captain, left marching, his gaze directed towards the viewer. In the background, marching soldiers. Two lines of Latin under the picture. Counterpart of the picture of the standard-bearer in 1587.

5) P.72 Portrait of a man with a banner in his left hand. Identified as Gerrit Pietersz. Ruychaver. Simple background and margin under the picture are left blank.

▲ ▶ *Rudolph's army soldiers from Goltzius artwork*

Tympanotriba peditum Hisp.   *Tibicen legionarius Hisp.*   *Prafectus milium, quem vel corporatum vulgo Vocant, vel Sargantum.*   *Signiferi Hisp. habitus.*

II

6) P.73 - A man with a musket (gun type) over the left shoulder and a furket (musket fork) in the right hand, in a nutshell. In the background a burning windmill and a soldier chasing a woman out of her house. Among the show two lines of text in Latin. This print is part of a series of three military officers.

7) P.74 - A man with a sword in his left hand and a shield in his right, seen from the back. In the background soldiers.

8) P.75 - Full length portrait of a Polish nobleman, probably Stanislas Sobocki, at the age of 27, the left hand side, right hand on his staff captain. He visited in 1583, when he was with a Polish delegation in the Netherlands, Goltzius in Haarlem to paint her portrait. At the top right of the presentation a coat of arms with a motto. In the background fray. Among the show's space left empty for a signature. See also the portrait of the Somlyó Balthasar Bathory, the leader of the delegation.

9) P.76 - Full length portrait of the Polish nobleman Balthasar Bathory Somlyó at the age of 22, the right hand side, left hand on the hilt of the sword at his side. He visited in 1583, when he was with a Polish delegation in the Netherlands, Goltzius in Haarlem to paint her portrait. At the top right of the presentation a coat of arms with a motto. In the background fray. Among the show's space left empty for a signature. See also the portrait of Stanislas Sobocki, a member of the delegation.

10) P.77 - Portrait of a man holding a banner over his right shoulder. It is unclear who he is; when identifications are named C. Wetthem Gerrit Cornelisz. Velserman and Gerrit van Schooten Jansz., Ensign Haarlem. In the background a battle. Among the show a four-line poem French.

11) P.78 - Portrait of a man (probably) a partisan (pole weapon) in his left hand. Previously also identified as Gerrit de Jong, N. Block or Peter Dz. Hasselaer. In the background a battle. Among the show a four-line poem Dutch.

12) P.79 - Portrait of a man (probably) a partisan (pole weapon) in his left hand. An infantry officer. In the background a battle. Among the show two lines of Latin.

13) P.80 - A man in military gear (a lieutenant colonel), in a nutshell, a sword at his belt, a stick weapon (partisan) in his right hand. In the background, a hilly landscape in which a city is besieged. Among the show two lines of text in Latin. This print is part of a series of 12 numbered prints of soldiers, full length displayed against a scenic background in which military operations are carried out, and with a two-line caption Latin. Probably a work of de ghyn on the stile of Glotzius.

14) P.81 - A man in military gear (a sergeant), full length, seen on the left, a sword at his belt, a stick weapon (halberd) in his right hand. In the background, a hilly landscape in which a siege. Among the show two lines of text in Latin. This print is part of a series of 12 numbered prints of soldiers, full length displayed against a scenic background in which military operations are carried out, and with a two-line caption Latin.

15) P.82 - A man with a spear in his left hand and a sword on the left side (a lieutenant), full length, seen on the right side. In the background a city with a harbor. Among the show two lines of text in Latin.

16) P.83 - A man in military gear (peaking kidney), full length, seen on the left, a sword at his belt, a stick weapon (peak or spear) in his right hand. In the background, a hilly landscape in which a troop of soldiers marching. Among the show two lines of text in Latin. This print is part of a series of 12 numbered prints of soldiers, full length displayed against a scenic background in which military operations are carried out, and with a two-line caption Latin.

17) P.84 - A man with a big drum to his left and a stick in his raised right hand (a drummer), full length, seen from the back. In the background, a hilly landscape in which a troop of soldiers marching. Among the show two lines of text in Latin. This print is part of a series of 12 numbered prints of soldiers, full length displayed against a scenic background in which military operations are carried out, and with a two-line caption Latin.

18) P.85 - A man in military gear (a colonel), full length, seen on the left, a sword at his belt, a stick weapon (partisan) in his right hand. In the background, a hilly landscape where a stroke occurs. Among the show two lines of text in Latin. This print is part of a series of 12 numbered prints of soldiers, full length displayed against a scenic background in which military operations are carried out, and with a two-line caption Latin.

19) P. 86 - A man with a staff in his right hand (a provost), in a nutshell, a sword at his belt. In the background a soldier cuffed away. Among the show two lines of text in Latin. This print is part of a series of 12 numbered prints of soldiers, full length displayed against a scenic

background in which military operations are carried out, and with a two-line caption Latin.

20) P.87 - A soldier with a rifle (musket) and a lighted wick in his left hand and a furketstok in the right hand, in a nutshell. In the background, a hilly landscape where soldiers shoot each other. Among the show two lines of text in Latin. This print is part of a series of 12 numbered prints of soldiers, full length displayed against a scenic background in which military operations are carried out, and with a two-line caption Latin.

21) P.88 - A soldier with a rifle (musket or harquebus) over the left shoulder, a burning wick in the right hand and a sword on the left side, in a nutshell, seen from the back. In the background a landscape where soldiers shoot each other. Among the show two lines of text in Latin. This print is part of a series of 12 numbered prints of soldiers, full length displayed against a scenic background in which military operations are carried out, and with a two-line caption Latin.

22) P.89 - A soldier with a rifle (harquebus) and a lighted wick in his left hand and a sword on the left side, in a nutshell. In the background, a hilly landscape where soldiers patrol. Among the show two lines of text in Latin. This print is part of a series of 12 numbered prints of soldiers, full length displayed against a scenic background in which military operations are carried out, and with a two-line caption Latin.

23) P.90 - A soldier with a sword in his right hand and a shield in his left hand, in a nutshell. In the background, a hilly landscape in which a troop of soldiers marching. Among the show two lines of text in Latin. This print is part of a series of 12 numbered prints of soldiers, full length displayed against a scenic background in which military operations are carried out, and with a two-line caption Latin.

24) P.91 - A man with a big banner over his left (a standard-bearer), full length, seen on the right. In the background, a hilly landscape in which a troop of soldiers marching. Among the show two lines of text in Latin. This print is part of a series of 12 numbered prints of soldiers, full length displayed against a scenic background in which military operations are carried out, and with a two-line caption Latin.

25) P.92 - A man carrying a rolled up piece of paper in his right hand (the treasurer), full length, seen on the left, a sword at his belt. In the background an army camp in which a treasurer of a large crate at a table in the open air makes payments to soldiers. Among the show two lines of text in Latin. This print is part of a series of 12 numbered prints of soldiers, full length displayed against a scenic background in which military operations are carried out, and with a two-line caption Latin.

26) P.93 - Portrait of a soldier with spear and sword in a nutshell. In the background is seen the siege of a city. Under the portrait of a fresh two lines about the loyalty of the soldier signed C.P. This last artwork was not realized by Goltzius.

Le
MANIEMENT D'ARMES
DE NASSAV,
a'vecq
Rondelles, Piques, Espees,
& Targes;

Representez par Figures, selon le nouveau ordre du Tresillustre Prince

MAVRICE de NASSAV,
Gouverneur, Admiral, & Cappitanie Gene-
ral des Provinces Vnies du pays bas, &c.
Par
ADAM van BREEN,
Avecq Instruction par escript pour tons Cappitai-
nes & Commandeurs, nouvellement mis
en lumiere.

IMPRIME Anno 1618,
A la Haye en Hollande, avecq Previlege de la Mat. Imperiale, & du
Roy Treschristien de France, aussi des Hault & puissans Seigneurs
les Estats Generaulx des Provinces Vnies du pays bas.
Ex Officina Arnoldi Meuris.

ADAM VAN BREE COLOUR PLATES

*

SOLDIERS OF THE PRINCE OF NASSAU

A.V. Breen Inventor.

2

3

6

7

8

25

9

12

14

15

16

17

20

21

22

23

24

25

26

27

28

29

30

31

2

4

7

8

11

13

HENDRICK GOLTZIUS COLOUR PLATES

*

THE IMPERIAL RUDOLPH'S ARMY

Mortales fugitis mortem? patriamq̃ tueri
Horretis pauidi? mors suaq̃ queng̃ manet
Vita nimis nulli placeat quem mors terit vsq̃.
Qui si HODIE est aliquid, CRAS NIHIL esse potest.

Signifer ingentes animos, et corda ministro,
Me stat stante phalanx, me fugiente fugit.

Hæltzius excud.

Laudata ducibus præstat succumbere morte,
Quàm vitæ turpi consuluisse metu.

A° 1587. HGoltzius fecit

Prœuius infractos reddo Dux Martis alumnos,
Spernere dum doceo cuncta perida, meo.

Pro patria pugnans, armis hostemꝗ lacessens
Officio fungor sedulus vsꝗ meo.

S.S. ÆTAT. 27.

ET NATVRA ET ARTE. 1585.

Kiloskus fecit

75

B.B.D.S. ÆTAT. 22.

Voyant Voſtre angelycque face,
Je puis dire pour le myeulx.
En pardomant mon audace,
Que sans vous AVLTRE NE VEVLX,
DE WETTHEM.

Des lants weluaert, moet zyn bewaert, byden getrouwen,
Die aen elcken cant, voor tvaderslant, haer trouw bewysen
Daermen int begin, sonder gewin, op mochten bouwen,
Sulck een men plach, DIE NOCH TOE SACH, lofflick te pryfen.
Harman Adolfz. excudit. Haerlemensis.

Ioannes Casimirus comes Palatinus Rheni
Dux Bauariæ ætatis 42. anno 1578.

Præuius infractos reddo Dux Martis alumnos,
Spernere dum doceo cuncta pericla, meo.

Mr. Jnu Ahaf v londerfel excudit

Munus ego absentis Ducis expleo, et alter ab illo
Jure Locum teneo, iure capesso vicem

Ante ferox Signanus ago promptum agmen ad arma,
Haudᵹ parum debent parta trophæa mihi.

Laudata ducibus preſtat ſuccumbere morte,
Quàm vitæ turpi conſuluiſſe metu

Goltzius fecit 1589   Boſſcher excu

9 Hr. excud. Eŏem sculp.

Conferto turbare acies forte agmine amicas
Si paret hoftis atrox, noftra Sariffa vetat.

I. de. Gheyn fculp.   HG. inue.

Suta boum pulſo ſimul ac mea Tympana pelle,
Miles ad excubias promptus et arma ruit.   3

Hiolt-zius. Jnuent. et excud. A° 1587.   Iacpnes de Gheyn: ſculp.

Militię Caput, et magnum inter prelia fulmen,
Infracta auſbicys pectora reddo meis .

1.

P. Kr. excu.   I. de gheijn sculp~

Effrænes belli prauosqᵹ coerceo motus,
Vindice me miles dum sibi vincla tunet.

_I._ _HE. excut._ _I. de gheyn. sculp._

Et genus, et mea me virtus terraq́ mariq́
Non imo patitur nomen habere loco.

Jussus in hostiles cuneos, noctuq; dieq;
Peruigil, indomito robore pronus agor.

6.   *Hi. exud. Kilyn sculp.*

Auertunt frandem mea Symbola, et hostis iniqui
Argutos remouet cautio nostra dolos.

5   HE inu XL excut

Dupla ega pro meritis mereor stipendia; nempe
Insigni reliquis strenuitate prior

HK. excud. Iacques de gheyn sculp.

4 Acer in aduersos tendo dum Signifer hostes,
   Martiolis crescit spesq́, animisq́ vigor.

Jo. Hr. excud. Isiegn sculp.

Tempore si numerem promptè stipendia certo,
Impauidos animos Martia turba capit.

Des Landts weluaert Moet Syn Bewaet Door desen die an
ElckenCant Voor Tuaderlandt Haer troubewysen.   C.P.

Effranes belli priuusq́ coerceo motus,
Vindict me miles dum sibi vincla tunet.